I0489022

1

Unique Heart Mandala Designs For Adults

Artistic Heart Mandala Coloring Books for Adults

Heart Mandala

By : Gala Publication

2

Published By :

Gala Publication
© Copyright 2015 – Gala Publication

ISBN-13: **978-1522722380**
ISBN-10: **1522722386**

Design 1

Design 2

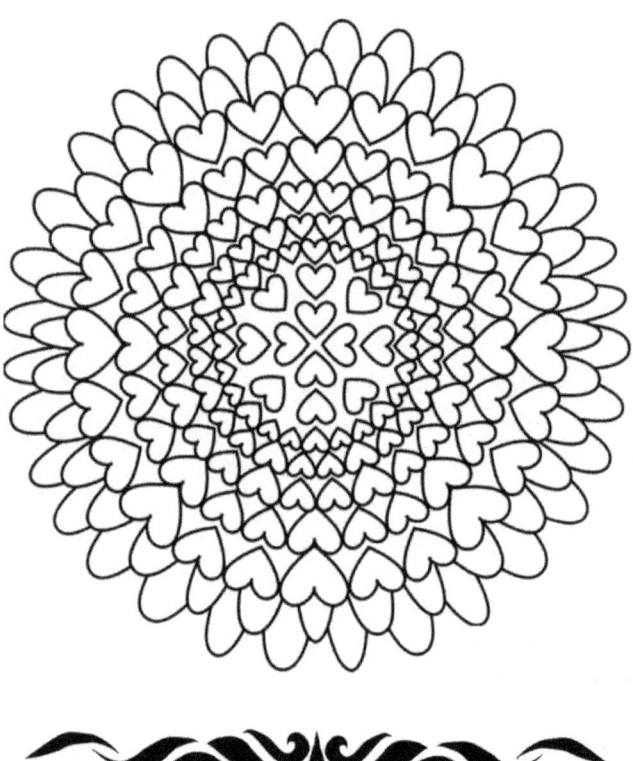

Design 3

Design 4

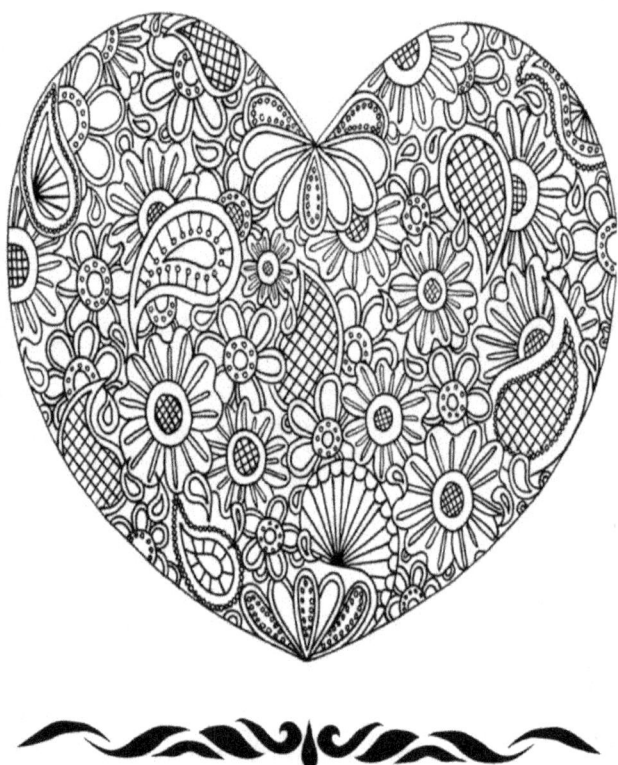

Design 5

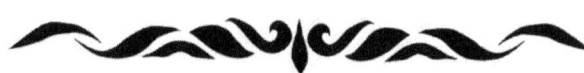

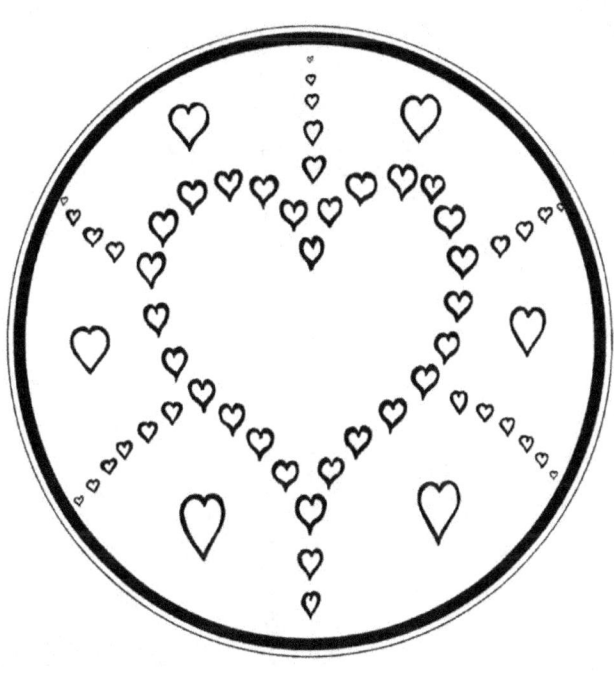

Design 6

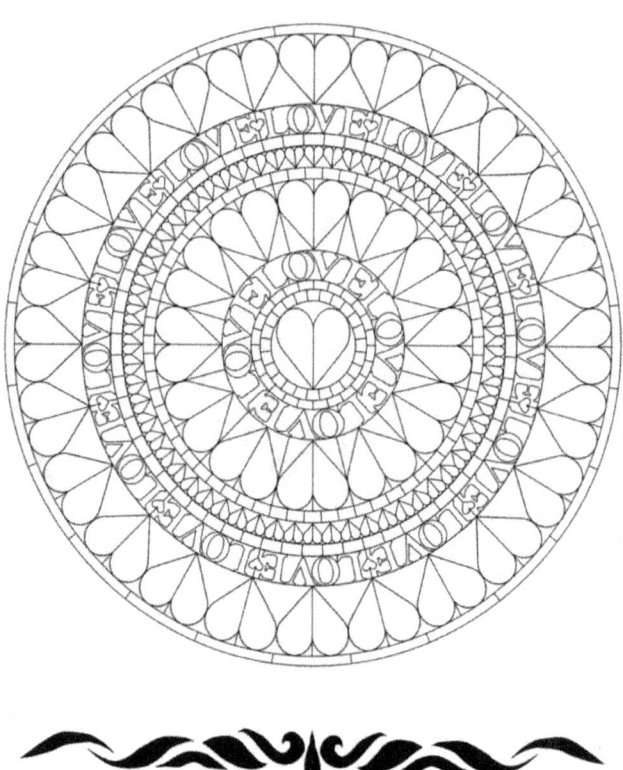

Design 7

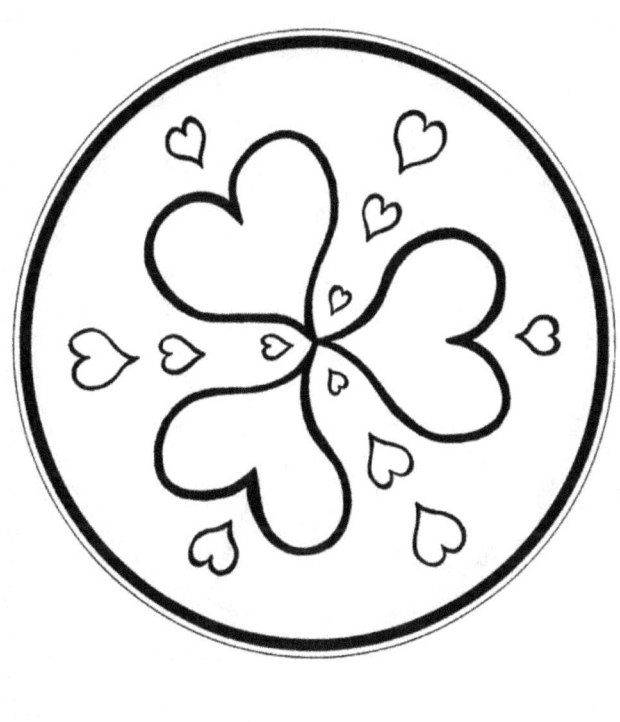

Design 8

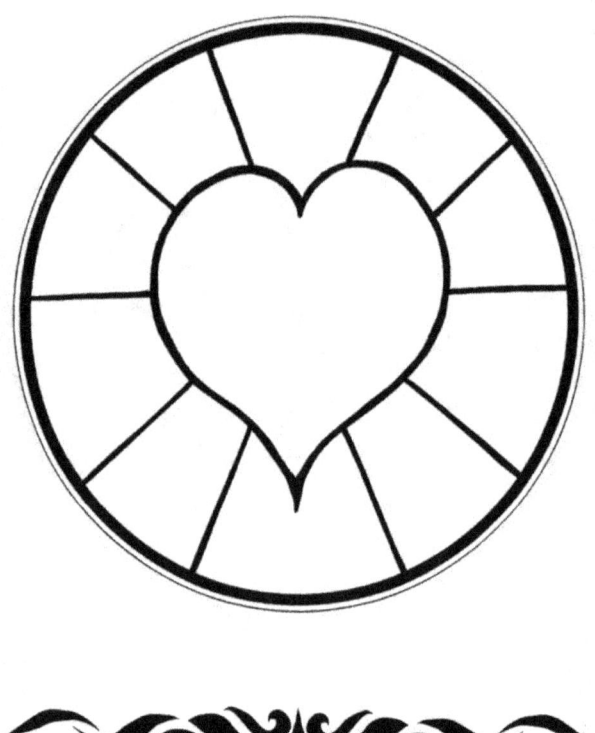

Design 9

Design 10

Design 11

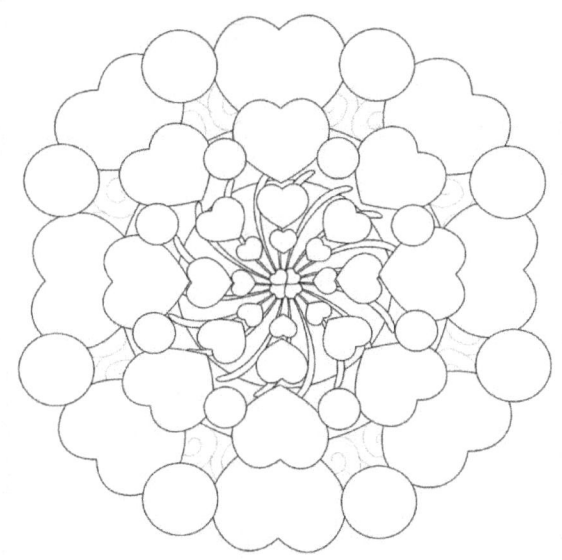

Design 12

Design 13

Design 14

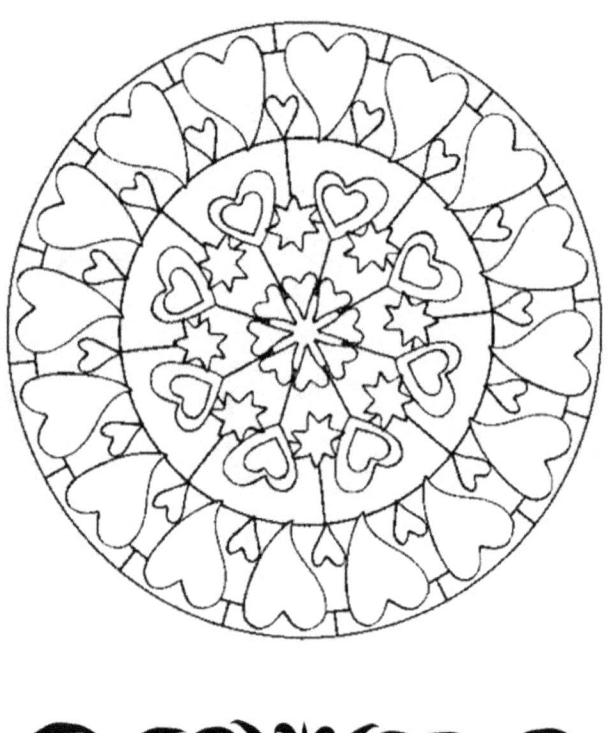

Design 15

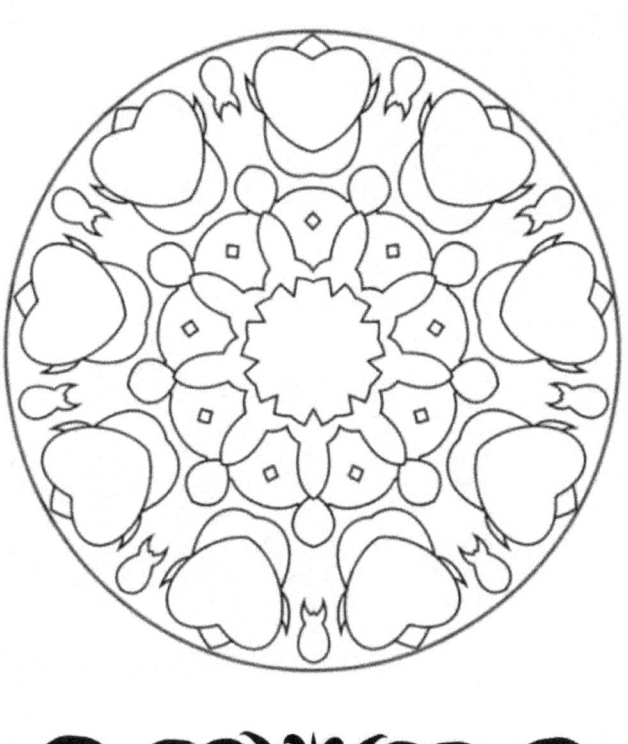

Design 16

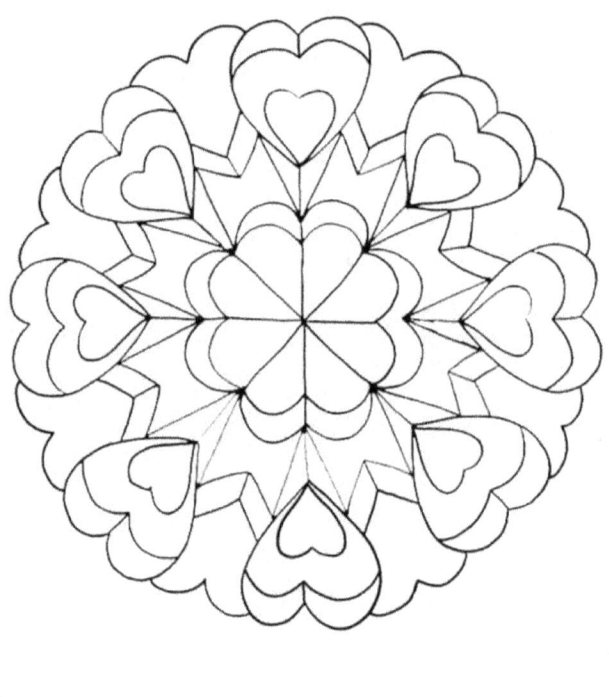

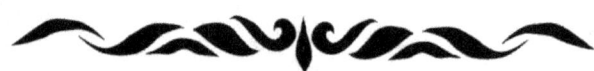

Design 17

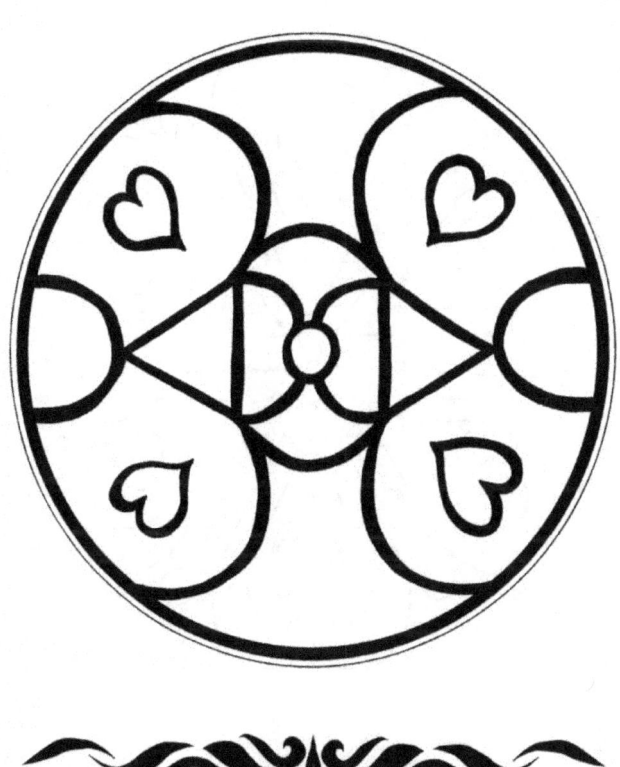

Design 18

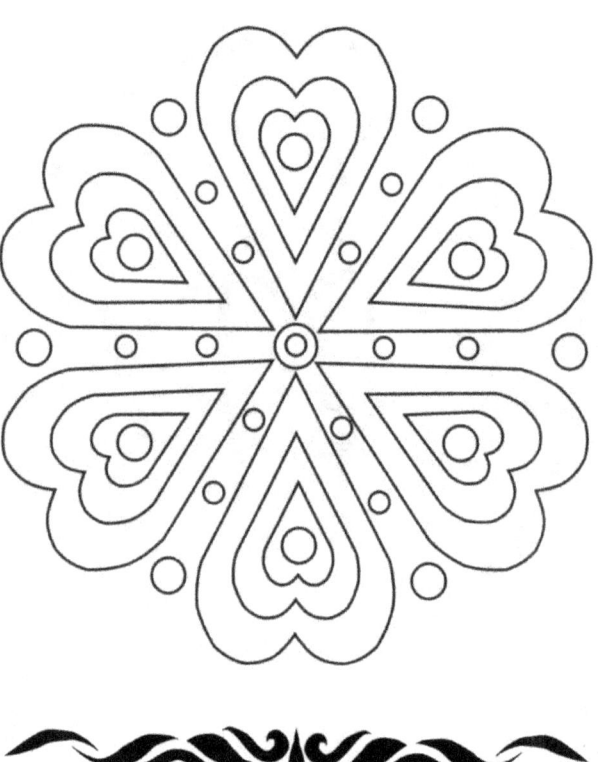

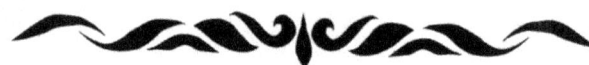

Design 19

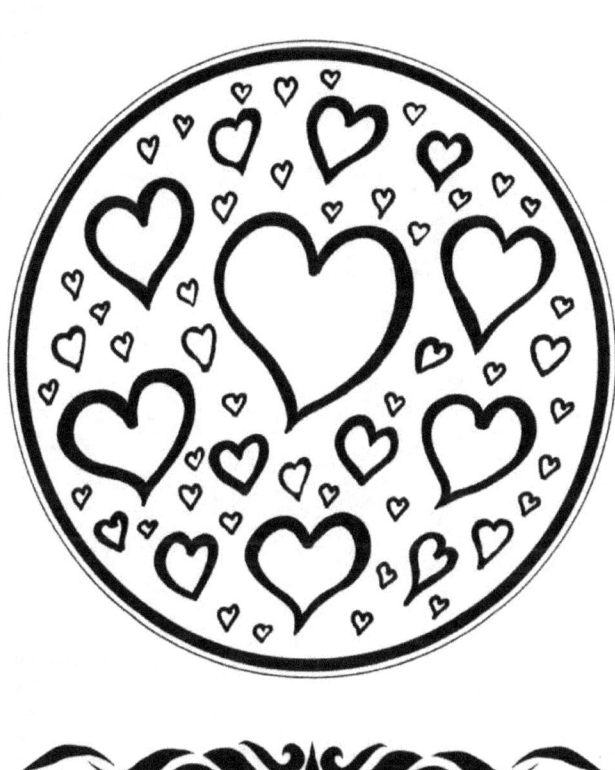

Design 20

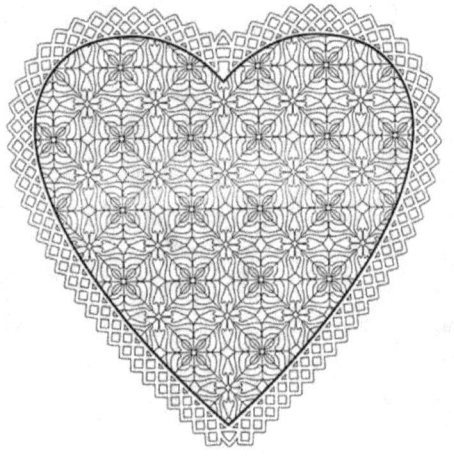

Design 21

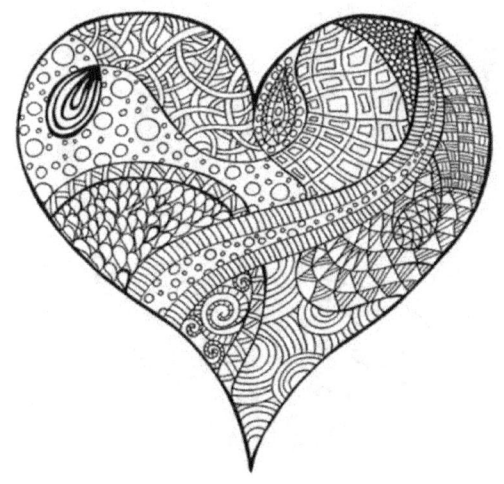

Design 22

Design 23

Design 24

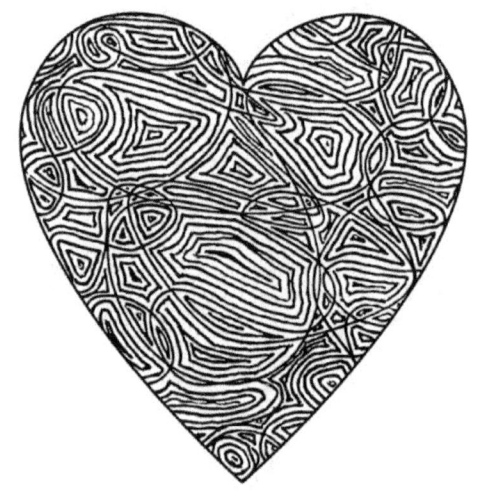

Design 25

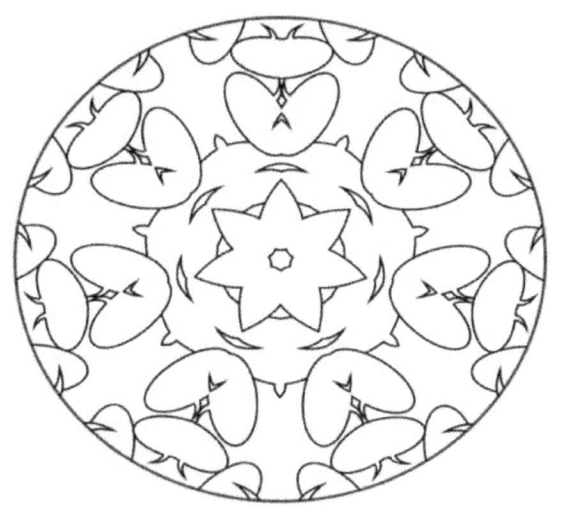